NORTH AMERICA'S
BIGGEST
BEASTS

MOOSE

Amy B. Rogers

PowerKiDS
press

New York

Published in 2016 by The Rosen Publishing Group, Inc.
29 East 21st Street, New York, NY 10010

First Edition

Editor: Katie Kawa
Book Design: Reann Nye

Photo Credits: Cover (background) RIRF Stock/Shutterstock.com; cover (moose), p. 1 Greg Winston/National Geographic/Getty Images; p. 4 NancyS/Shutterstock.com; p. 5 Tom Reichner/Shutterstock.com; p. 6 Erik Mandre/Shutterstock.com; pp. 7, 20 Pictureguy/Shutterstock.com; p. 8 S.J. Krasemann/Photolibrary/Getty Images; p. 9 BGSmith/Shutterstock.com; p. 10–11 Chris Rubino/Shutterstock.com; p. 12 Wild Art/Shutterstock.com; p. 13 Frontpage/Shutterstock.com; p. 14 Iussiya/Shutterstock.com; p. 15 TheGreenMan/Shutterstock.com; p. 16 Ronnie Howard/Shutterstock.com; p. 17 Robert O Hull/Shutterstock.com; p. 18 mlorenz/Shutterstock.com; p. 19 Africa Studio/Shutterstock.com; p. 21 Marc Schlossman/Photographer's Choice/Getty Images; p. 22 Eastcott Momatiuk/DigitalVision/Getty Images.

Cataloging-in-Publication Data

Rogers, Amy B.
Moose / by Amy B. Rogers.
p. cm. — (North America's biggest beasts)
Includes index.
ISBN 978-1-5081-4296-6 (pbk.)
ISBN 978-1-4994-1852-1 (6-pack)
ISBN 978-1-5081-4301-7 (library binding)
1. Moose — Juvenile literature. I. Rogers, Amy B. II. Title.
QL737.U55 R58 2016
599.65'7—d23

Manufactured in the United States of America

CPSIA Compliance Information: Batch #BW16PK: For Further Information contact Rosen Publishing, New York, New York at 1-800-237-9932

CONTENTS

Mighty Moose 4

A Look at Antlers. 6

A Body Built for the Cold 8

Staying Cool 10

Running and Swimming. 12

Fighting for Females 14

Big Babies 16

Eating and Being Eaten 18

A Big Danger 20

Looking for Moose. 22

Glossary 23

Index. 24

Websites 24

Mighty Moose

Different kinds of deer can be found all over North America. However, one species, or kind, of deer stands out from the rest of its animal family because of its size. The moose is the largest species of deer in the world!

An adult male moose can weigh over 1,300 pounds (589.7 kg). They can stand over 6 feet (1.8 m) tall at the shoulder. The biggest moose are often found in Alaska, but these massive **mammals** live in cold places throughout North America.

THE BIG IDEA

"Moose" is a name that's only used in North America. In Europe, moose are called "elk."

A moose is much bigger than a person! People who live near moose like to look at these big deer, but they also know to give them plenty of space.

A Look at Antlers

Most people can spot a moose by its antlers. These are the bony horns on the head of a deer. Only male moose, which are called bulls, have antlers. Females, which are called cows, never grow them. Bulls lose their antlers every winter and grow them back in the spring.

Moose have huge antlers! Their antlers can grow to be over 6 feet (1.8 m) wide. Bulls use their antlers to fight each other for **mates**. Antlers also help bulls fight off predators.

bull

cow

It's easy to tell a male moose from a female. Bulls are generally larger than cows, and bulls are the only moose that have antlers.

A Body Built for the Cold

A moose's big body is built for life in cold weather. Moose have thick fur that can be many different shades of brown—from golden to almost black. A moose's head is long, and it has a flap of skin called a bell that hangs beneath its throat.

A moose also has four strong hoofs, each of which has two toes. These hoofs support a moose's body when it walks in the snow or mud. They act like snowshoes to keep the moose from sinking.

moose hoof

THE BIG IDEA

Moose sometimes leave hoof prints, or tracks, in the ground when they walk. These tracks are each split down the middle. They're generally between 4 and 6 inches (10.2 and 15.2 cm) long and between 3 and 5 inches (7.6 and 12.7 cm) wide.

Moose have two dewclaws on the back of each of their legs, near each hoof. A dewclaw is like an extra toe that doesn't touch the ground.

dewclaw

9

Staying Cool

Moose make their home in some of the coldest parts of North America. They live in the northern parts of the **continent**, including Alaska and Canada. They're also found in the northeastern United States and in parts of the **Rocky Mountains** as far south as Colorado.

Moose live in cold places because their large bodies get very hot, and they don't sweat to cool themselves down. They also often live near ponds and streams, which they swim in during warmer months to stay cool.

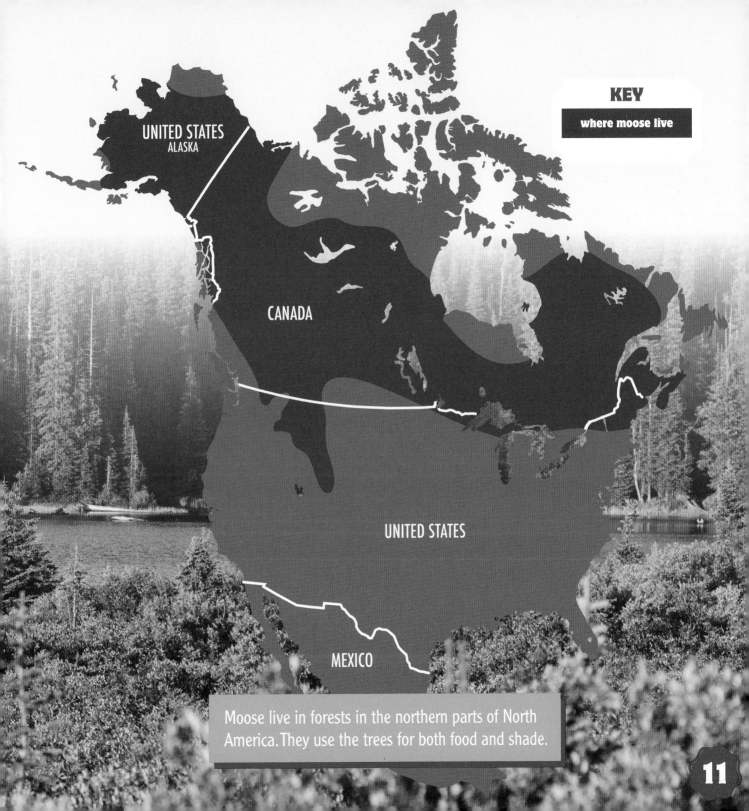

UNITED STATES
ALASKA

CANADA

UNITED STATES

MEXICO

Moose live in forests in the northern parts of North America. They use the trees for both food and shade.

Running and Swimming

Moose use their strong hoofs to walk around their snow-covered **habitats** in the winter. Their long legs help them walk through the snow, too. Those long legs are also good for running at high speeds. Moose can run as fast as 35 miles (56.3 km) per hour. That's fast for any animal, but it's especially fast for an animal as large as a moose.

Moose are also good swimmers. They can swim for miles at a time at speeds of up to 6 miles (9.7 km) per hour.

Moose like to swim. They can even go completely underwater!

Fighting for Females

You won't see too many moose running or swimming together. Moose are solitary animals, which means they spend most of their time alone. However, moose gather in groups during their mating season, which happens every fall.

Cows and bulls call to each other using loud sounds when it's time to mate. Then, bulls fight each other over the cows, using their antlers. Bulls sometimes get hurt during these fights. It's not easy getting poked, scratched, and hit with such large antlers!

After the bulls fight each other, they mate with the cows. Once the mating season is over, bulls and cows go their separate ways until the following fall.

Big Babies

After the fall mating season, cows have their babies in late spring. They generally only have one or two babies, which are called calves, at one time. Calves are born big! They can weigh over 30 pounds (13.6 kg) at birth. Calves then gain about 3 pounds (1.4 kg) a day while drinking milk from their mother.

A calf can run faster than a person less than a week after it's born. Calves stay with their mother until the next mating season. Their mother teaches them how to **survive** on their own.

THE BIG IDEA

Of all moose, calves are most in danger of being hunted by predators. Up to half of all calves die before they're a year old.

Moose don't usually stay around other moose, but it's different for cows and calves. The strongest bond between moose is the bond between a mother and her babies.

Eating and Being Eaten

Moose are herbivores, which means they only eat plants. They eat tall grasses because they're so tall. Moose also eat twigs, tree bark, and leaves. In the winter, they eat from **coniferous** trees such as fir trees. In the summer, they eat water plants, such as water lilies.

Moose can be food for other animals. Healthy adult moose aren't often hunted by predators. However, calves, old moose, and sick moose are at risk. Predators that hunt these moose include wolves, brown bears, and black bears.

THE BIG IDEA

Moose need to eat over 44 pounds (20 kg) of food every day!

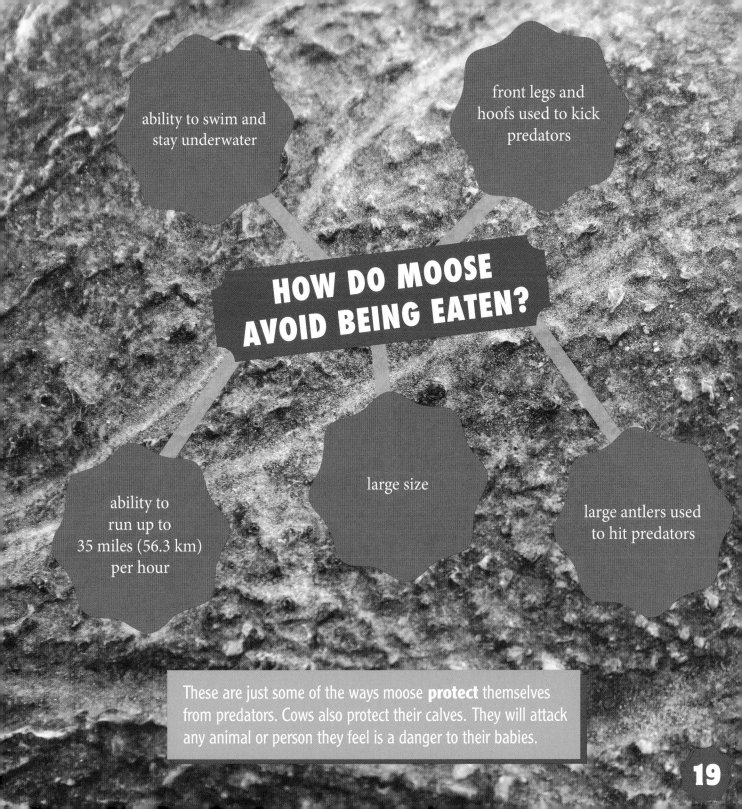

ability to swim and stay underwater

front legs and hoofs used to kick predators

HOW DO MOOSE AVOID BEING EATEN?

ability to run up to 35 miles (56.3 km) per hour

large size

large antlers used to hit predators

These are just some of the ways moose **protect** themselves from predators. Cows also protect their calves. They will attack any animal or person they feel is a danger to their babies.

A Big Danger

People are one of the biggest dangers to moose populations in North America. Moose hunting for sport is very popular in some areas. Humans have taken away moose habitats when they build in places that were once forests. Moose are also killed by cars, and sometimes this can hurt or kill the people in the cars, too.

A moose will attack a person if it believes that person could harm it. People have been hurt and even killed in moose attacks throughout North America.

THE BIG IDEA

Moose are also hunted for their meat. In Alaska, one adult moose can give a hunter as much as 500 pounds (226.8 kg) of meat.

Road signs throughout Canada and northern parts of the United States warn drivers to look out for moose.

Looking for Moose

Moose are mighty mammals that can swim for miles, run at high speeds, and kick with enough force to hurt predators. With their big body and antlers, they're easy to see. If you're ever in a forest where moose might live, you can look for moose tracks in the mud or snow with help from an adult. If you see any, a moose might be nearby.

If you see a moose, don't get too close. It's much safer to watch these big deer from far away!

Glossary

coniferous: Referring to a bush or tree that produces cones and leaves, called needles, that are green all year.

continent: One of the seven great masses of land on Earth.

habitat: The natural home for plants, animals, and other living things.

mammal: Any warm-blooded animal whose babies drink milk and whose body is covered with hair or fur.

mate: One of a pair of male and female animals that come together to make babies. Also, to come together to make babies.

protect: To keep safe.

Rocky Mountains: The main mountain system in western North America that extends from Alaska to New Mexico.

survive: To keep living.

Index

A

Alaska, 4, 10, 11, 20
antlers, 6, 7, 14,
     19, 22

B

bell, 8
bulls, 6, 7, 14, 15

C

calves, 16, 17,
     18, 19
Canada, 10, 11, 21
Colorado, 10
cows, 6, 7, 14, 15,
     16, 17, 19

D

deer, 4, 5, 6, 22
dewclaws, 9

F

fight, 6, 14, 15
food, 11, 18

H

herbivores, 18
hoofs, 8, 9, 12, 19
hunt, 16, 18, 20

M

mammals, 4, 22
mating, 14, 15, 16

P

predators, 6, 16, 18,
     19, 22

R

Rocky
     Mountains, 10

S

swimming, 10, 12,
     13, 14, 19, 22

T

tracks, 8, 22

Websites

Due to the changing nature of Internet links, PowerKids Press has developed an online list of websites related to the subject of this book. This site is updated regularly. Please use this link to access the list: www.powerkidslinks.com/nabb/moose